The Victoria and Albert Museum

WILLIAM MORRIS

Pocket Diary 1997

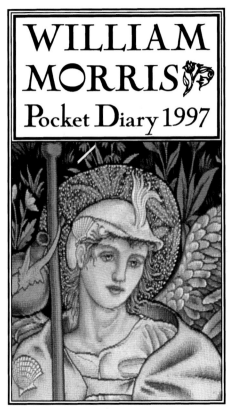

EBURY PRESS STATIONERY

PERSONAL DETAILS

Name _____

Address _____

Telephone (home) _____ (business) _____

First published in the United Kingdom in 1996 by Ebury Press Stationery
Random House, 20 Vauxhall Bridge Road, London SW1V 2SA
Random House UK Limited Reg. No. 954009

Whilst every effort has been made to ensure accuracy,
the publishers cannot accept liability for errors.

Warning: Clauses in the Banking and Financial Dealings Act
allow the Government to alter dates at short notice.

Calendarial and Astronomical data included in this diary is supplied by
HM Nautical Almanac Office © Copyright
Particle Physics and Astronomy Research Council.

Set in Cochin/Caslon by SX Composing Ltd, Rayleigh, Essex
Printed in Hong Kong
Designed by David Fordham

ISBN 0 09 181267 4

The V&A Patrons offer the Museum's highest level of corporate and private
support. For information, please contact The Development Office
on 0171 938 8271

For information on joining the Friends of the V&A
contact the Friends Office on 0171 589 4040

MUSEUM HOURS OF OPENING
Monday 12 noon – 17.50 Tuesday – Sunday 10.00 – 17.50
Closed Christmas Eve, Christmas Day, Boxing Day and New Year's Day

January
M	T	W	T	F	S	S
		1	2	3	4	5
6	7	8	9	10	11	12
13	14	15	16	17	18	19
20	21	22	23	24	25	26
27	28	29	30	31		

February
M	T	W	T	F	S	S
					1	2
3	4	5	6	7	8	9
10	11	12	13	14	15	16
17	18	19	20	21	22	23
24	25	26	27	28		

March
M	T	W	T	F	S	S
31					1	2
3	4	5	6	7	8	9
10	11	12	13	14	15	16
17	18	19	20	21	22	23
24	25	26	27	28	29	30

April
M	T	W	T	F	S	S
	1	2	3	4	5	6
7	8	9	10	11	12	13
14	15	16	17	18	19	20
21	22	23	24	25	26	27
28	29	30				

May
M	T	W	T	F	S	S
			1	2	3	4
5	6	7	8	9	10	11
12	13	14	15	16	17	18
19	20	21	22	23	24	25
26	27	28	29	30	31	

June
M	T	W	T	F	S	S
30						1
2	3	4	5	6	7	8
9	10	11	12	13	14	15
16	17	18	19	20	21	22
23	24	25	26	27	28	29

July
M	T	W	T	F	S	S
	1	2	3	4	5	6
7	8	9	10	11	12	13
14	15	16	17	18	19	20
21	22	23	24	25	26	27
28	29	30	31			

August
M	T	W	T	F	S	S
				1	2	3
4	5	6	7	8	9	10
11	12	13	14	15	16	17
18	19	20	21	22	23	24
25	26	27	28	29	30	31

September
M	T	W	T	F	S	S
1	2	3	4	5	6	7
8	9	10	11	12	13	14
15	16	17	18	19	20	21
22	23	24	25	26	27	28
29	30					

October
M	T	W	T	F	S	S
	1	2	3	4		
		1	2	3	4	5
6	7	8	9	10	11	12
13	14	15	16	17	18	19
20	21	22	23	24	25	26
27	28	29	30	31		

November
M	T	W	T	F	S	S
					1	2
3	4	5	6	7	8	9
10	11	12	13	14	15	16
17	18	19	20	21	22	23
24	25	26	27	28	29	30

December
M	T	W	T	F	S	S
1	2	3	4	5	6	7
8	9	10	11	12	13	14
15	16	17	18	19	20	21
22	23	24	25	26	27	28
29	30	31				

January
M	T	W	T	F	S	S
			1	2	3	4
5	6	7	8	9	10	11
12	13	14	15	16	17	18
19	20	21	22	23	24	25
26	27	28	29	30	31	

February
M	T	W	T	F	S	S
						1
2	3	4	5	6	7	8
9	10	11	12	13	14	15
16	17	18	19	20	21	22
23	24	25	26	27	28	

March
M	T	W	T	F	S	S
30	31					1
2	3	4	5	6	7	8
9	10	11	12	13	14	15
16	17	18	19	20	21	22
23	24	25	26	27	28	29

April
M	T	W	T	F	S	S
		1	2	3	4	5
6	7	8	9	10	11	12
13	14	15	16	17	18	19
20	21	22	23	24	25	26
27	28	29	30			

May
M	T	W	T	F	S	S
				1	2	3
4	5	6	7	8	9	10
11	12	13	14	15	16	17
18	19	20	21	22	23	24
25	26	27	28	29	30	31

June
M	T	W	T	F	S	S
1	2	3	4	5	6	7
8	9	10	11	12	13	14
15	16	17	18	19	20	21
22	23	24	25	26	27	28
29	30					

July
M	T	W	T	F	S	S
		1	2	3	4	5
6	7	8	9	10	11	12
13	14	15	16	17	18	19
20	21	22	23	24	25	26
27	28	29	30	31		

August
M	T	W	T	F	S	S
31					1	2
3	4	5	6	7	8	9
10	11	12	13	14	15	16
17	18	19	20	21	22	23
24	25	26	27	28	29	30

September
M	T	W	T	F	S	S
	1	2	3	4	5	6
7	8	9	10	11	12	13
14	15	16	17	18	19	20
21	22	23	24	25	26	27
28	29	30				

October
M	T	W	T	F	S	S
			1	2	3	4
5	6	7	8	9	10	11
12	13	14	15	16	17	18
19	20	21	22	23	24	25
26	27	28	29	30	31	

November
M	T	W	T	F	S	S
30						1
2	3	4	5	6	7	8
9	10	11	12	13	14	15
16	17	18	19	20	21	22
23	24	25	26	27	28	29

December
M	T	W	T	F	S	S
1	2	3	4	5	6	
7	8	9	10	11	12	13
14	15	16	17	18	19	20
21	22	23	24	25	26	27
28	29	30	31			

WILLIAM MORRIS
(1834-1896)

WILLIAM MORRIS is best known today as a designer of patterns. To his contemporaries he was better known as a poet. He was certainly a complex man, full of temper and contradictions, fired by enormous energies.

Born into wealth he married out of his class for love and for beauty. The failure and continuing unhappiness of his marriage meant he confided in two women, Aglaia Coronio and Georgiana Burne-Jones, herself trapped in an unhappy marriage.

Having rejected the priesthood, the career his parents preferred for him, he tried and discarded architecture and then painting, before founding his own firm to make and sell decorations for the home, succeeding as the model Victorian entrepreneur. He tried many crafts, most of them successfully, including stone and wood carving, illuminating, carpet, silk, and tapestry weaving. He was also a lecturer, polemicist, conservationist, botanist, historian, bibliophile, editor, traveller, translator, philosopher, socialist, publisher, designer, and more. He was also a practical man, never happier than when doing, trying for himself the processes of making, typically emerging stained with dye and sweat at the end of long days.

As his business grew he saw society had to change and that it could only be changed by revolution. His politics dealt with the immediate, contemporary issues of domestic and foreign policy as well as the past. His was a romantic vision of a chivalric, hierachical and religious England in the Middle Ages. His writings also looked to London in the twenty-first century, searching as always for certainties, looking for something more than the dehumanising horrors of the industrial present.

Few now read the poetry or the politics. It is the patterns which are loved, imitated and reprinted. Based on nature, closely, lovingly observed, and on historic examples which he found in, and collected for his Museum, his patterns have survived the test of time.

STEPHEN ASTLEY
Collection of Prints, Drawings and Paintings
Victoria and Albert Museum

MONDAY
30

___

TUESDAY
31

___

WEDNESDAY
1   Holiday (New Year's Day)

___

THURSDAY
2   ☽

___

FRIDAY
3

___

SATURDAY
4

___

SUNDAY
5

___

January

Epiphany

MONDAY
6

TUESDAY
7

WEDNESDAY
8

● THURSDAY
9

First Day of Ramadan (subject to sighting of the moon)   FRIDAY
10

SATURDAY
11

SUNDAY
12

January

MONDAY
13

TUESDAY
14

WEDNESDAY
15

THURSDAY
16

FRIDAY
17

SATURDAY
18

SUNDAY
19

REDCAR CARPET
Original sketch design. Watercolour. The carpet is in
the Victoria and Albert Museum.

January

MONDAY
20   Holiday, USA (Martin Luther King Jr's Birthday)

___

TUESDAY
21

___

WEDNESDAY
22

___

THURSDAY   ○
23

___

FRIDAY
24

___

SATURDAY
25

___

SUNDAY   Australia Day
26

January · February

Holiday, Australia (Australia Day)

MONDAY
27

TUESDAY
28

WEDNESDAY
29

THURSDAY
30

◑ FRIDAY
31

SATURDAY
1

SUNDAY
2

February

MONDAY
3

TUESDAY
4

WEDNESDAY
5

THURSDAY   Holiday, New Zealand (Waitangi Day)
6

FRIDAY   ●
7

SATURDAY
8

SUNDAY
9

SCROLL

Tile by William Morris, 1868-70. Morris & Co.

February

MONDAY
10

TUESDAY
11   Shrove Tuesday

WEDNESDAY
12   Ash Wednesday

THURSDAY
13

FRIDAY
14   ◑

SATURDAY
15

SUNDAY
16

February

Holiday, USA (President's Day)

MONDAY
17

TUESDAY
18

WEDNESDAY
19

THURSDAY
20

FRIDAY
21

○ SATURDAY
22

SUNDAY
23

MONDAY
24

TUESDAY
25

WEDNESDAY
26

THURSDAY
27

FRIDAY
28

SATURDAY   St David's Day
1

SUNDAY   ◐
2

PIMPERNEL

Wallpaper by William Morris. Colour print from wood
blocks.

March

MONDAY
3

TUESDAY
4

WEDNESDAY
5

THURSDAY
6

FRIDAY
7

SATURDAY
8

SUNDAY
9

● Mother's Day, UK

March

Commonwealth Day

MONDAY
10

TUESDAY
11

WEDNESDAY
12

THURSDAY
13

FRIDAY
14

SATURDAY
15

◑

SUNDAY
16

March

MONDAY
17

Holiday, Northern Ireland
(St Patrick's Day)

TUESDAY
18

WEDNESDAY
19

THURSDAY
20

Vernal Equinox, Spring Begins

FRIDAY
21

SATURDAY
22

SUNDAY
23

Palm Sunday

Thou rememberest how of old
Een thy very pain grew cold,
How thou mightst not measure bliss
Een when eyes and hands drew nigh.
Thou rememberest all regret
For the scarce remembered kiss,
The lost dream of how they met,
Mouths once parched with misery
Then seemed Love born but to die,
Now unrest, pain, bliss are one,
Love unhidden and alone.

LOVE FULFILLED

From *A Book of Verse* by William Morris. Written and
illustrated for Lady Georgiana Burne-Jones, 1870.

March

MONDAY ○
24

TUESDAY
25

WEDNESDAY
26

THURSDAY
27

FRIDAY   Holiday exc USA (Good Friday)
28

SATURDAY
29

SUNDAY   Easter Day
30   British Summer Time Begins, UK

March · April

◑ Holiday exc Scotland, USA

TUESDAY
1

WEDNESDAY
2

THURSDAY
3

FRIDAY
4

SATURDAY
5

DST Begins, USA

SUNDAY
6

April

MONDAY
7

●

TUESDAY
8

WEDNESDAY
9

THURSDAY
10

FRIDAY
11

SATURDAY
12

SUNDAY
13

DAISY

Wallpaper by William Morris, 1862, from the pattern
book of Morris & Co.

April

MONDAY
14

TUESDAY
15

WEDNESDAY
16

THURSDAY
17

FRIDAY
18

SATURDAY
19

SUNDAY
20

April

Birthday of Queen Elizabeth II

○ First day of Passover (Pesach)

St George's Day

Holiday, Australia, New Zealand (Anzac Day)

April · May

MONDAY
28

___

TUESDAY
29

___

WEDNESDAY
30   ◗

___

THURSDAY
1

___

FRIDAY
2

___

SATURDAY
3

___

SUNDAY
4

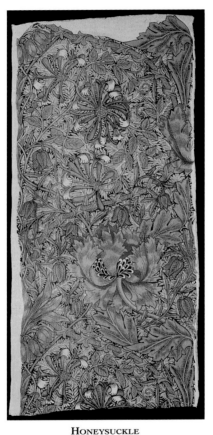

HONEYSUCKLE

Furnishing fabric by William Morris. Printed silk.
Printed by Thomas Clarkson, 1875-6.

May

MONDAY
5

Holiday, UK (tbc)

TUESDAY
6

●

WEDNESDAY
7

THURSDAY
8

Ascension Day

FRIDAY
9

Islamic New Year

SATURDAY
10

SUNDAY
11

May

MONDAY
12

TUESDAY
13

◑

WEDNESDAY
14

THURSDAY
15

FRIDAY
16

SATURDAY
17

Whit Sunday

SUNDAY
18

May

MONDAY
19   Holiday, Canada (Victoria Day)

TUESDAY
20

WEDNESDAY
21

THURSDAY
22   ○

FRIDAY
23

SATURDAY
24

SUNDAY
25   Trinity Sunday

EMBROIDERED PANEL

By William Morris or Edward Burne-Jones, c.1860.
Unfinished figure of a woman, probably Phyllis Wools,
painted on linen.

May · June

MONDAY
26

Holiday, UK
Holiday, USA (Memorial Day)

TUESDAY
27

WEDNESDAY
28

THURSDAY
29

◗ Corpus Christi

FRIDAY
30

SATURDAY
31

SUNDAY
1

June

Coronation Day
Holiday, NZ (Queen's Birthday)

MONDAY
2

TUESDAY
3

WEDNESDAY
4

● THURSDAY
5

FRIDAY
6

SATURDAY
7

SUNDAY
8

June

MONDAY
9

TUESDAY
10   Birthday of Prince Philip, Duke of Edinburgh

WEDNESDAY
11   Feast of Weeks (Shavuot)

THURSDAY
12

FRIDAY
13   ◖

SATURDAY
14

SUNDAY
15   Father's Day, UK and USA

SUNFLOWER

Embroidered panel. William Morris, 1876.
Embroidered in silks on linen by Catherine Holiday.

June

MONDAY
16

TUESDAY
17

WEDNESDAY
18

THURSDAY
19

FRIDAY   ○
20

SATURDAY   Summer Solstice, Summer Begins
21

SUNDAY
22

June

MONDAY
23

TUESDAY
24

WEDNESDAY
25

THURSDAY
26

FRIDAY
27

SATURDAY
28

SUNDAY
29

June · July

MONDAY
30

TUESDAY
1   Holiday, Canada (Canada Day)

WEDNESDAY
2

THURSDAY
3

FRIDAY
4   ● Holiday, USA (Independence Day)

SATURDAY
5

SUNDAY
6

TRELLIS

Wallpaper, 1862. Wood block print. This was William
Morris's first wallpaper design and Philip Webb drew
the birds. The idea was probably taken from hedges of
roses on wattlework at the Red House (the residence of
William Morris).

July

MONDAY
7

TUESDAY
8

WEDNESDAY
9

THURSDAY
10

FRIDAY
11

SATURDAY
12

◗ Battle of the Boyne

SUNDAY
13

July

Holiday, Northern Ireland (tbc)

MONDAY
14

TUESDAY
15

WEDNESDAY
16

THURSDAY
17

FRIDAY
18

SATURDAY
19

○

SUNDAY
20

July

MONDAY
21

TUESDAY
22

WEDNESDAY
23

THURSDAY
24

FRIDAY
25

SATURDAY
26   ◑

SUNDAY
27

FIGURE OF A WOMAN

Glass panel designed by Edward Burne-Jones and
William Morris and made by Morris & Co., 1860.

MONDAY
28

TUESDAY
29

WEDNESDAY
30

THURSDAY
31

FRIDAY
1

SATURDAY
2

SUNDAY
3

●

August

MONDAY
4

TUESDAY
5

WEDNESDAY
6

THURSDAY
7

FRIDAY
8

SATURDAY
9

SUNDAY
10

August

MONDAY ◗
11

TUESDAY
12

WEDNESDAY
13

THURSDAY
14

FRIDAY
15

SATURDAY
16

SUNDAY
17

WOVEN TAPESTRY DESIGN
Stylized foliage in a pale colour on a darker ground,
interspersed with birds and flowers.
By William Morris.

August

MONDAY
18   ○

___

TUESDAY
19

___

WEDNESDAY
20

___

THURSDAY
21

___

FRIDAY
22

___

SATURDAY
23

___

SUNDAY
24

August

◖ Holiday, UK

MONDAY
25

TUESDAY
26

WEDNESDAY
27

THURSDAY
28

FRIDAY
29

SATURDAY
30

SUNDAY
31

September

MONDAY
1

● Holiday, USA (Labor Day)
Holiday, Canada (Labour Day)

TUESDAY
2

WEDNESDAY
3

THURSDAY
4

FRIDAY
5

SATURDAY
6

SUNDAY
7

LILY AND POMEGRANATE
Wallpaper by William Morris. Wood block print.

September

MONDAY
8

TUESDAY
9

WEDNESDAY
10   ◐

THURSDAY
11

FRIDAY
12

SATURDAY
13

SUNDAY
14

September

MONDAY
15

TUESDAY
16

WEDNESDAY
17

THURSDAY
18

FRIDAY
19

SATURDAY
20

SUNDAY
21

September

MONDAY
22   Autumnal Equinox, Autumn Begins

TUESDAY
23   ◑

WEDNESDAY
24

THURSDAY
25

FRIDAY
26

SATURDAY
27

SUNDAY
28

TEXTILE

Copy of a Coptic textile. Tapestry of woven wool.
Morris & Co., *c.*1910.

September · October

MONDAY
29

TUESDAY
30

WEDNESDAY ●
1

THURSDAY   Jewish New Year (Rosh Hashanah)
2

FRIDAY
3

SATURDAY
4

SUNDAY
5

October

MONDAY
6

TUESDAY
7

WEDNESDAY
8

◐

THURSDAY
9

FRIDAY
10

Day of Atonement (Yom Kippur)

SATURDAY
11

SUNDAY
12

October

MONDAY
13

Holiday, USA (Columbus Day)
Holiday, Canada (Thanksgiving Day)

TUESDAY
14

WEDNESDAY
15

THURSDAY
16

○ First Day of Tabernacles (Succoth)

FRIDAY
17

SATURDAY
18

SUNDAY
19

VINE

Design for wallpaper by William Morris, 1873-4.
Pencil and watercolour.

October

MONDAY
20

TUESDAY
21

WEDNESDAY
22

THURSDAY
23   ◑

FRIDAY
24

SATURDAY
25

SUNDAY
26   British Summer Time Ends, UK
                                             DST Ends, USA

October · November

Holiday, New Zealand (Labour Day)

MONDAY
27

TUESDAY
28

WEDNESDAY
29

THURSDAY
30

● FRIDAY
31

SATURDAY
1

SUNDAY
2

November

MONDAY
3

TUESDAY
4

WEDNESDAY
5

THURSDAY
6

FRIDAY   ◐
7

SATURDAY
8

SUNDAY   Remembrance Sunday
9

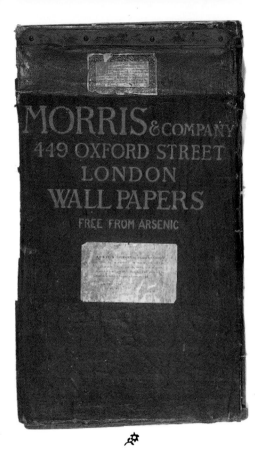

FRONT COVER OF WALLPAPER STAND BOOK

Wooden easel stand, leatherette cover. Contains wall
paper samples. Morris & Co., *c.*1905.

November

MONDAY
10

TUESDAY
11
Holiday, USA (Veterans' Day)
Holiday, Canada (Remembrance Day)

WEDNESDAY
12

THURSDAY
13

FRIDAY
14
○ Birthday of the Prince of Wales

SATURDAY
15

SUNDAY
16

November

MONDAY
17

TUESDAY
18

WEDNESDAY
19

THURSDAY
20

FRIDAY
21

SATURDAY
22

SUNDAY
23

November

WEEK 48

MONDAY
24

TUESDAY
25

WEDNESDAY
26

THURSDAY
27

Holiday, USA (Thanksgiving Day)

FRIDAY
28

SATURDAY
29

SUNDAY
30

● First Sunday in Advent
St Andrew's Day

The Pigeon
Embroidered panel by J H Dearle. Morris & Co., 1898

December

MONDAY
1

TUESDAY
2

WEDNESDAY
3

THURSDAY
4

FRIDAY
5

SATURDAY
6

SUNDAY   ◗
7

December

MONDAY
8

TUESDAY
9

WEDNESDAY
10

THURSDAY
11

FRIDAY
12

SATURDAY
13

○ SUNDAY
14

December

MONDAY
15

___

TUESDAY
16

___

WEDNESDAY
17

___

THURSDAY
18

___

FRIDAY
19

___

SATURDAY
20

___

SUNDAY
21　　　　　　　◗ Winter Solstice, Winter Begins

DESIGN FOR AN EMBROIDERED PANEL
Done by William Morris for the Red House, Bexley,
Kent (his own home), depicting a female figure wearing
a crown and holding a torch, inscribed "Flamma
Troiae", c.1860. Pencil and watercolour.

December

MONDAY
22

TUESDAY
23

WEDNESDAY
24

Christmas Eve
First Day in Hanukah

THURSDAY
25

Christmas Day

FRIDAY
26

Holiday exc USA (Boxing Day)

SATURDAY
27

SUNDAY
28

December · January 1998

●

MONDAY
29

TUESDAY
30

First Day of Ramadan

WEDNESDAY
31

Holiday (New Year's Day)

THURSDAY
1

FRIDAY
2

SATURDAY
3

SUNDAY
4

Addresses

NAME

ADDRESS

TELEPHONE

NAME

ADDRESS

TELEPHONE

NAME

ADDRESS

TELEPHONE

NAME

ADDRESS

TELEPHONE

NAME

ADDRESS

TELEPHONE

TEXTILE

Copy of a Coptic textile. Tapestry of woven wool.
Morris & Co., *c.*1910.

Addresses

NAME

ADDRESS

TELEPHONE

NAME

ADDRESS

TELEPHONE

NAME

ADDRESS

TELEPHONE

NAME

ADDRESS

TELEPHONE

NAME

ADDRESS

TELEPHONE

Addresses

NAME

ADDRESS

TELEPHONE

NAME

ADDRESS

TELEPHONE

NAME

ADDRESS

TELEPHONE

NAME

ADDRESS

TELEPHONE

NAME

ADDRESS

TELEPHONE

CARICATURE

Morris reading his poetry to Burne-Jones.

Front cover and title page: "Angeli Ministrantes" (detail). Tapestry designed by William Morris and Edward Burne-Jones, 1894. Originally drawn for stained glass windows in Salisbury Cathedral. Back cover: "The Orchard" (detail). Tapestry designed by William Morris and J H Dearle. Woven by Morris & Co., 1890.